Hadrian's Wall

Roger Clegg

HADRIAN'S WALL
C O U N T R Y

Published by Northern Heritage Services Ltd 2024

Units 7&8 New Kennels, Blagdon Estate, Seaton Burn
Newcastle upon Tyne, NE13 6DB
Telephone 01670 789940

NORTHERN
HERITAGE

www.northern-heritage.co.uk

Text and photography copyright:
© 2024 Roger Clegg
Text edited by Paul Frodsham

Design and Layout:
© 2024 Ian Scott Design

Printed and bound in China by Latitude Press Limited
British Library Cataloguing in Publication Data
A catalogue record for this book is available from the British Library.
ISBN: 978-1-7394861-0-5

Acknowledgements

Thanks to English Heritage, National Trust, The Vindolanda Trust, Northumberland National Park, Tyne and Wear Museum Services and the many custodians along the Wall.

This book is dedicated to my wife Lin.

Hadrian's Wall

Roger Clegg

Foreword
by LJ Ross

In the realm of visual storytelling, few canvases are as evocative and steeped in history as the landscapes surrounding Hadrian's Wall. It is here, amidst the rolling hills and timeless vistas, that Roger Clegg has set his lens to capture moments of transcendent beauty and profound historical significance. As an author who has often found inspiration in these very landscapes, it is both an honour and a privilege to write the foreword for this magnificent collection.

Roger's work is more than just photography; it is a portal into the heart of Northumberland, inviting us to step through the frame into a world where the past and present coalesce in a dance of light and shadow. His images are imbued with the spirit of the land, each shot a story whispered by the winds that sweep across the ancient Roman Wall.

When I first saw the photograph that would become the emblem of my second DCI Ryan novel, "Sycamore Gap," I was struck by the raw emotion it evoked. Roger has a unique ability to encapsulate the essence of a place, to distil its story into a single, breathtaking snapshot. His vision brings the landscape to life, each photo a testament to his profound connection with the region and his skill as a master craftsman of the lens.

Hadrian's Wall country is a region of contrasts and surprises, where history's echo is felt in every stone and every turn of the path brings a new revelation. Roger Clegg's work captures this spirit perfectly, each photograph a celebration of the land's rugged beauty and its enduring legacy.

To leaf through the pages of this book is to embark on a journey through time and space, guided by Roger's unerring eye for detail and composition. Whether you are a lover of history, a fan of natural beauty, or simply someone who appreciates the art of photography, this collection is sure to inspire and delight.

As you immerse yourself in these images, I hope you will feel, as I do, the profound sense of connection to this extraordinary part of the world. Roger Clegg's photography is not just a visual feast; it is a love letter to Hadrian's Wall country, penned in light and shadow.

With admiration and respect,
LJ Ross
Author of the DCI Ryan Series

Sycamore Gap

CONTENTS

Hadrian's Wall Country

This is a book about a large area of the northern border counties of England. It has appropriately become known as 'Hadrian's Wall Country' and stretches from the North Sea to the Solway Firth, including parts of the counties of Tyne and Wear, Northumberland and Cumbria. It also includes the two great cities of Newcastle upon Tyne and Carlisle.

It is a land of grand hills and big rivers dominated by the River Tyne and its tributaries - the River North Tyne and the River South Tyne. The River North Tyne rises in hills and solitude near the Anglo-Scottish Border – for centuries a wild, dangerous, and most inhospitable place to live. It flows through the huge reservoir of Kielder Water and on to the village of Bellingham where it turns in a southerly direction through North Tynedale. Just to the west of Hexham, near the village of Warden, it reaches Watersmeet, the confluence with its southern counterpart, the River South Tyne.

The River South Tyne begins its ever-changing journey high on Cross Fell in Cumbria, the highest and most remote hill in the North Pennines. It tumbles down the steep moorland slopes gathering water as it hurries its way to Garrigill and on to Alston, a small, picturesque market town with a very steep main street. Flowing north, the river widens and slows as it passes through mainly livestock farmland between the hills of South Tynedale to the small historic town of Haltwhistle. Continuing east for fifteen miles its journey ends where it meets the River North Tyne to create the mighty River Tyne, which flows for a further thirty-one miles to the North Sea at Tynemouth.

Starting in the east, the course of Hadrian's Wall runs through urban Tyneside with its focal point of Newcastle/Gateshead. Newcastle upon Tyne is a beautiful and historic city noted for engineering and innovation, including the world-changing development of reliable and fast steam locomotion. In a world not confined by imposed boundaries of specialisation, the Stephensons built not only locomotives but complete railway systems including spectacular viaducts and bridges. Newcastle has been for centuries a centre of medical innovation and with its exceptional hospitals and the Centre for Life continues this tradition today. Gateshead, just across the Tyne, is a centre for the arts with the Glasshouse International Centre for Music (previously the Sage) and the Baltic Centre for Contemporary Art.

Continuing westwards, Tyneside gives way to England's most sparsely populated county – Northumberland! Northumberland is a place of big skies, big hills, big rivers and one mighty big historic monument - Hadrian's Wall. To get away from the stresses and strains of life there can be nowhere better. South of Hadrian's Wall the River South Tyne and its tributaries provide an area of farmland before the North Pennines moorland takes over. North of Hadrian's Wall is a large very sparsely populated area of hills, rivers and Kielder Water leading to the Scottish Border – if you enjoy solitude, again, there is no better place.

Looking south from the central section of Hadrian's Wall is a land of big skies and distant views – especially in the central section looking over South Tynedale. In midsummer the sky will remain light until midnight.

The central section of Hadrian's Wall is characterised by undulating crags with frequently precipitous north faces along the line of the Whin Sill. The Whin Sill, formed by volcanic action about 300 million years ago, passes through Northumberland and County Durham and can be seen at spectacular locations such as Lindisfarne, Bamburgh and Dunstanburgh castles in North Northumberland, and High Force waterfall in Upper Teesdale, County Durham.

Hadrian's Wall Country is an area that has probably seen more violence and warfare than any other part of Britain. The Wall itself has a complex history which can't be considered in any detail here (see below for some recommended books about it). Its construction was ordered by the emperor Hadrian in the 120s to help manage the northern frontier of the mighty Roman empire, extending from here to the Sahara desert. The original plan seems to have been for a mighty wall from coast to coast, with access through it restricted (with a small number of exceptions) to milecastles (located approximately one Roman mile apart), between which were two interval turrets at roughly regular intervals. Behind the Wall lay the Vallum, a huge earthwork probably intended to create a 'military corridor' between it and the Wall. During construction, however, the plans were changed, and several mighty forts were added to the line. Despite all this investment, Roman rule in Britain came to an end in the early fifth century, after which northern England suffered invasions by Anglo-Saxons, Vikings and eventually (after 1066) Normans.

The medieval Anglo-Scottish wars resulted in many castles being built in Hadrian's Wall Country. These include Newcastle in the east and Carlisle in the west, along with many others such as Thirlwall which made good use of recycled Roman stone (as indeed do numerous churches, farmhouses and even field walls). Later in date than the castles are the numerous bastles, such as that built within the south gateway of Housesteads fort. These date to the era of the infamous Border Reivers. Reiver clans, extending to both sides of the border, took advantage of the lack of law and order to attack and rob each other, perpetuating feuds and revenge raids. The reiving clans were known as 'Names', and many

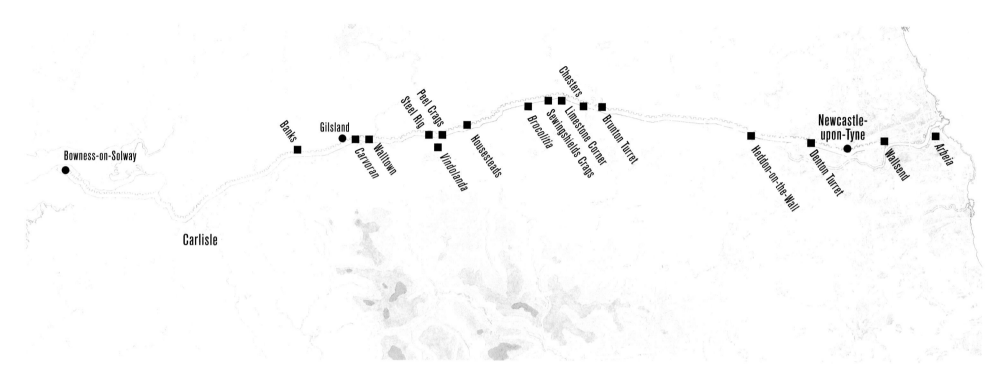

of these names persist in Hadrian's Wall Country as today's surnames. Eventually, following the Union of the Crowns, peace broke out along the border, leading to the expansion of settlements, agricultural improvement, and today's tranquil landscape that belies its violent past.

It is estimated that about seven thousand people a year accept the challenge of 'Walking the Wall' from Coast to Coast. The more athletic and physically fit may even choose to run it! A considerably larger number visit the Wall with more leisurely intentions. Access to Hadrian's Wall is easy. For those with a car there are many car parks giving good access to enjoy the beauty and the drama of the landscape. For those using public transport there are the Hadrian's Wall AD122 buses that link with Hexham and Haltwhistle railway stations. The bus timetables change significantly according to the time of year – always check when planning your visit. Accommodation is abundant to suit all needs of comfort and price, ranging from bunk houses and camp sites to B&Bs and high quality hotels. There are many well-informed guides available who offer guided tours to enhance your enjoyment of all or part of Hadrian's Wall and maybe areas beyond.

Hadrian's Wall is now a UNESCO World Heritage Site that includes many of Britain's finest and most-visited Roman sites. Many Roman forts are open to the public along the length of the Wall, and many historic reenactments are held each year, including some specifically for children during the school holidays. In addition to the well-known sites, there are numerous beautiful little valleys that remain virtually unexplored, many of them hiding secret walks and waterfalls.

Hadrian's Wall Country has something for everyone, but, perhaps more importantly, it offers a unique combination of space and secret corners where the pressures of today's overcrowded lifestyle can be put aside, at least for a while.

Why photograph Hadrian's Wall?

At the time of creating this book I will have been living in Hexham, about five miles from Hadrian's Wall, for 34 years. Steeped in history and legend this famous monument runs through the most varied, beautiful and frequently dramatic scenery from lowland pastures and salt marsh to the wild and exposed upland crags of the Whin Sill fault. It also includes the two famous cities of Newcastle-upon-Tyne and Carlisle. I suspected that most people know of Hadrian's Wall but relatively few know much about this most intriguing and spectacular historic monument including exactly where it is. It is frequently referred to as the current English - Scottish border. In fact, in the east the Scottish border is seventy miles north of Hadrian's and in the west ten miles north of Carlisle.

The history of Hadrian's Wall and immediate area is amazing. Much has been extremely violent, particularly after the departure of the Romans with the eras of the invading Vikings, Border Reivers and the Scottish / English War. In contrast to the violence, innovation has been prolific. Perhaps the greatest being Robert and George Stevenson who took the erratic, unreliable and cumbersome technology of early steam locomotion and set it on course for the railways we know today. An achievement that literally changed the world for ever by making fast, safe, affordable transport over long distances.

My job, brilliant as it was had become unsustainable – with medical advice I had to give it up! I had enjoyed photography as a relaxation for many years so I thought it was time to give it a go seriously. My first attempt at selling my pictures was an education and a major set back! Not that I had any problems with selling, I had been in sales for many years. As I placed my slides on the light box in front of my first potential customer, something suddenly made itself very obvious – most of my pictures of Hadrian's Wall did not actually feature Hadrian's Wall - I had pictures taken of the scenery on the other side of the Wall with my elbows on the Wall to steady the camera. I had pictures taken at the bottom of the crags obscuring the Wall on the top of the crags, and pictures where the Wall was so small you could hardly see it - and so on.

When I looked at other photographers' pictures and their successes there was no hiding place – mine were bland, boring and meaningless! This was not a good start! A rude

awakening! Time to take things seriously or get out before even starting! I really had to get my act together and take a good, long, hard look at how to produce pictures provoking the reaction "Wow! Where is that?".

This precipitated my photographic "road to Damascus". The scales fell from my eyes. When photography was an escape from an extremely demanding job, enjoying the process of photography was more enjoyable than the quality of the resulting picture. Producing a book was a different matter.

How to get the best technically out of a camera was not a problem. Knowing what to do to take good pictures was not a problem. It was the application that was the stumbling block.

The first thing I did was to create a check list for taking good pictures. Top of the list was do not go out without a target to achieve. The check list went: History, Myth, Legend, Wilderness, Bleakness, Turbulence, Beauty, Drama, Solidity, Context, Purpose, Timelessness, Diversity, Difference. Every picture had to contain some of these criteria.

It may seem strange to say that much of my early photography of Hadrian's Wall Country is done at home. The time spent on planning is well worth it – by knowing where to go, combined with knowing when to go, why you are considerably increases your chances of success. Your photography then becomes much more enjoyable and rewarding.

I have three weather apps on my mobile phone – they all tend to give slightly different weather predictions! Between them they give a good indication of the expected weather for any particular location. I also have a sun compass. This will show me on a map, for anywhere I wish to stand, where the sun will rise or set. With these apps I can plan my photography knowing when to go to any location when the sun is in the right place considerably increasing my chance of getting the picture I want.

Carrying everything is an issue. Many, many years ago when I became really enthusiastic about my photography my photo bag could have two medium format cameras a number of heavy lenses, a heavy tripod, plus, vitally important, a tea making kit and

water – its weigh was intimidating. Now I carry a smaller high quality APS format camera plus two professional quality good zoom lenses and achieve as much if not more. I still take the most important component – the tea making kit. I usually go out before sunrise and when my photography is complete can enjoy a couple of mugs of tea and immerse myself in the beauty of the unfolding of new day.

I have derived great pleasure from my photography of Hadrian's Wall and the resulting pictures. To be present when the sun first appears as a pinpoint of light above the crags is always magical. To watch the mist and fog forming, gently undulating, waxing and waning in the hollows and at the base of the crags is spell binding. The sky forewarns you of the impending sunrise with changing, colour and brightness. The clouds set the mood with their bright warm colours, whether it be intense red, subtle pinks or orange. They can be ragged persued by a strengthening wind or delicate and static with the promise of a good day ahead. Sunset is also a magical spectacle but tends to lack some of the subtly of sunrise. Also, there is a greater chance of people being there removing the impression timelessness.

For the photographer Hadrian's Wall has much to offer. Two great cities, the fabulous Rivers Tyne, South Tyne and North Tyne and tributaries, woodland, moorland, the Northumberland National Park and, of course the Wall!

My photography has been used to promote Hadrian's Wall in the UK and world-wide as well as adorning the sides of buses and a train. Two images were used for a tremendously successful poster campaign in major London Underground stations. Another was used for a 10meter wide panoramic picture of Hadrian's Wall at the entrance to the British Museum. One of my pictures of Sycamore Gap was used in the television program to find Britain's Favourite Tree. It won the England section.

I have enjoyed my photography of Hadrian's Wall Country. I hope you get the same pleasure from looking at this book as I have in creating it.

Looking west from the Knag Burn Gate along the line of Housesteads Crags, Cuddy's Crags and Hotbank Crags at the end of a day of wet snow.

TYNESIDE

The excavated remains of
the Temple of Antenociticus
at Benwell.

Inside the reconstructed bath-house
at Segedunum fort, Wallsend.

The River Tyne, Newcastle Quayside and The Glasshouse, Gateshead, showing three of the five bridges over the Tyne in or near to the city centre.

The Theatre Royal and Grey Street. The historic area of Grainger Town has many important listed buildings.

The keep of Newcastle Castle is built on the remains of the Roman fort of Pons Aelius.

RIVER TYNE COUNTRY

Upstream of Newcastle, the River Tyne is transformed from an urban and once heavily polluted industrial river to a beautiful rural waterway.

George and Robert Stephenson lived in one room of this cottage in Wylam. A very modest beginning for the father and son who transformed the unreliable and cumbersome early attempts at steam locomotion into the world's first fast and reliable means of long distance transport.

Prudhoe Castle was constructed by the Normans during the 11th century and modified many times including the building of an Elizabethan Manor House within the castle walls. Tynedale was a dangerous place to be through many centuries and Prudhoe Castle was positioned high above the River Tyne to control one of the few easy crossing points.

CORBRIDGE
CORSTOPITUM

Located at the junction of Dere Street (the main Roman road from York up into Scotland) and the Stanegate (to Carlisle in the west), and above the north bank of the Tyne, Corbridge (Corstopitum, or Coria) was not a fort but a flourishing town and supply centre that catered for the occupants of the forts on Hadrian's Wall (which passes 4km to the north) and the local civilian population. It was occupied continuously from the late first century through until the end of Roman rule in the early fifth century. Because the village of Corbridge developed on a different site, to the east, much of the Roman town survived relatively undamaged, though much Roman masonry was 'recycled' for reuse elsewhere and the site was also damaged by ploughing. The site saw numerous excavations throughout the twentieth century, and today the consolidated ruins of various buildings, to either side of the Stanegate, can be visited, along with the splendid on site museum.

Two views of Aydon Castle, a splendid late thirteenth-century fortified manor-house located 2km north of Corbridge. Despite a turbulent history during the Border Wars, it survives remarkably intact.

HADRIAN'S WALL
EAST SECTION

The A69 from Carlisle, close to its junction with the A1.
Many people passing along this road are unaware of the
roadside ruins of one the world's great historic monuments.

Heddon-on-the-Wall is the first visible stretch of Hadrian's Wall as you travel westwards into Northumberland. The round structure is a kiln added several centuries after the end of Roman rule.

The earthworks of the vallum at Down Hill, high above the River Tyne, with the North Pennines in the distance.

The Hadrian's Wall Path approaching the site of Milecastle 24 (Wall Fell).

18

St Oswald's Church is believed to be the location of the Battle of Heavenfield; fought in 633 or 634, this was a defining battle in the development of the Northumbrian 'Golden Age' and of Christianity in northern England.

A bench against the north wall of the church offer a magnificent view across North Tynedale and distant hills - a perfect place to sit and enjoy a cup of tea or coffee.

In the soft light of a frosty autumn morning, this stile offers access to Brunton Turret and the River North Tyne.

Continuing our journey westwards, we arrive at Planetrees. The land drops away towards the River North Tyne revealing beautiful views across the hills of North Tynedale and Tynedale.

Planetrees on a day of light snow, highlighting the patchwork landscape of this part of North Tynedale.

Brunton Turret.

Chesters

Substantial remains of a cavalry fort, built astride Hadrian's Wall immediately west of the River North Tyne, can be seen today, along with an impressive bath-house. An extensive vicus (civil settlement) lay between the fort and the river; this has been surveyed using aerial imagery and geophysics, but not excavated. On the opposite side of the river, the abutment of the bridge that carried Hadrian's Wall across the river can be visited. The fascinating on-site museum includes Roman tombstones and other finds, from Chesters and elsewhere.

The abutments of the Roman bridge at Chesters, seen from the west bank of the North Tyne.

The bath-house for Chesters fort can be seen on the far (west) bank of the North Tyne, with remains of the bridge's east abutment in the foreground.

HADRIAN'S WALL
CENTRAL SECTION

Looking eastwards along Peel Crags from above
Milecastle 39 (Castle Nick) on a summer afternoon of
great clarity, with sunny spells and abnormally dark
threatening clouds.

After climbing up from Chesters, Hadrian's Wall reaches Black Carts where a substantial length of Wall, including the ruins of Turret 29a, still stands.

Looking north-east over the Wall at Black Carts, towards a stunning sunrise on a misty summer morning.

Running parallel to the Wall on its north side is a substantial defensive ditch, clearly visible in these winter morning views of Black Carts.

The Wall ditch at Black Carts, with the low sun backlighting the summer grasses.

Bright winter early morning sunlight emphasises the stone work of Hadrian's Wall.

Limestone corner on a warm,
hazy spring evening.

Limestone Corner is not as the name suggests. The rock is actually
quartz-dolerite whinstone which is much harder than limestone. This
is usually cited as the reason why the digging of the Wall ditch was
never completed here.

A panoramic view of North Tynedale from Limestone Corner.

A panoramic winter view of North Tynedale from Limestone Corner.

Sunset on a calm spring evening at Carrawburgh (Brocolitia).

Sunset at the mithraeum (temple of Mithras), Carrawburgh (Brocolitia).

Looking east over Sewingshields milecastle,
beneath a towering Northumberland sky.

The easternmost of the major Whin Sill crags is at Sewingshields, with panoramic views in all directions.

From the highest point on Sewingshields Crags, Hadrian's Wall drops steeply to Kennel Crags.

Ice-covered Greenlee Lough on a clear, freezing winter day.

Sewingshields Crags, approaching
Kennel Crags.

Drumlins sculpted by eastward-flowing glacial ice during the Ice Age.

Kennel Crags on a beautiful winter afternoon and autumn evening (opposite page). Busy Gap, at the bottom of the crags, was a popular overnight resting location in the days of the cattle droves from Scotland to Newcastle. Much livestock would mysteriously disappear overnight, due to the activities of the local 'Busy Gap rogues'.

Looking over the Knag Burn towards Housesteads fort. Where the Wall crosses the Knag Burn, there is a small gateway, the only gap of its type known along the whole length of the Wall, as gates were only provided at milecastles, forts and main roads. This presumably relates to the fact that the north gate of the fort was essentially inaccessible above Housesteads Crags.

The Knag Burn is a small stream flowing from an area of bog to the north of Housesteads fort which, even during long periods of little or no rain, never ceases to flow. It invites the question of how the garrison of the adjacent fort acquired its water. It seems likely that rainwater was collated into large stone tanks, but on some occasions this may have been supplemented by water from the Knag Burn.

Outside the fort's south are consolidated remains of the Vicus, the civilian settlement associated with the fort.

Housesteads

Housesteads is the best-known fort on the Wall, on account of its substantial excavated and consolidated remains and its splendid landscape setting. It is an infantry fort, built to house up to 1,000 men. Its north wall is on the line of Hadrian's Wall, which bonds with its north-west and north-east corners. The fort wall survives around the entire perimeter, and remains of all four main gateways can be seen. Within the fort can be seen the headquarters building, commanding officer's house, hospital, granaries, barrack blocks and a splendidly preserved latrine. There was a substantial vicus (civil settlement) outside the fort, a few buildings of which have been excavated and consolidated. The site museum displays many fascinating finds.

A view along the south wall of Housesteads fort, looking towards the south gate.

The latrines in the south-east corner of Housesteads fort.

The south gate at Housesteads, seen from within the fort. More than a thousand years after the end of Roman rule, in the late sixteenth century, a bastle house was built here, using recycled Roman masonry, by members of the notorious Armstrong clan.

Thick frost coats ruins of buildings within the fort, early on a freezing winter morning.

The remains of a pillar within the headquarters building at Housesteads, with a spectacular winter sunrise.

Looking east over the remnants of the Housesteads headquarters, towards a magnificent autumn sunrise.

Housesteads fort with a colourful autumn sunrise over the granaries.

The granaries at Housesteads fort, clearly showing the supporting pillars of the now-dismantled floor. The gap created by these pillars helped to keep food stored within the granaries dry and fresh.

The Housesteads granaries on a beautiful winter morning.

Autumn mists nestle in low-lying hollows of the undulating landscape, with ruins of the Housesteads headquarters building in the foreground.

Looking east along the north wall of Housesteads fort towards the Knag Burn Gateway, with Sewingshields Crags in the distance.

The plantation on Housesteads Crags on an exceptionally cold winter day. Thick rime ice has developed on branches exposed to the wind, while hoar frost covers more sheltered branches.

West of the fort, the Wall continues along Housesteads Crags through a small area of mixed woodland known as Housesteads Plantation.

A beautiful winter view of the plantation on Housesteads Crags.

Milecastle 37 (Housesteads) on a beautiful winter morning. Remnants of an internal building, thought to be a barrack block, can be seen.

Cuddy's Crags provide some of the most iconic views of Hadrian's Wall, here with Housesteads Crags, Kennel Crags and Sewingshields Crags all receding into the winter mist.

A view eastwards from Cuddy's Crags, surrounded by lush springtime vegetation, towards a dramatic sunrise.

Cuddy's Crags on a hazy spring morning.

A view eastwards along the Wall
from Cuddy's Crags towards
Housesteads Crags and beyond.

A thick hoar frost glowing in the failing light of a very cold winter evening on Hotbank Crags, with Housesteads Crags in the distance.

High on Hotbank Crags on a frosty evening, looking into a fine winter sunset.

Hotbank Crags on a warm spring evening, with Crag Lough and Winshield Crags in the distance.

The Wall dropping down Hotbank Crags to Crag Lough, seen on a cool early winter evening.

Viewed from Hotbank Crags, a shaft of late winter sun shines a dramatic spotlight on Crag Lough.

Hotbank Farm, at the base of Hotbank Crags, looking towards Crag Lough and Highshield Crags.

Crag Lough and Highshield Crags on a cool autumn evening, with Winshield Crags in the distance.

A ragged late winter sky over Highshield Crags, with low-lying mist on Crag Lough.

The pastel tones of a benign winter sky create a picture of serenity over Highshield Crags and Crag Lough.

Mist hugs the line of Peel Crags and Highshield Crags, beneath a fragmented but calm autumn sky.

A Spring sky of rare intensity over Hotbank Farm.

A bright winter morning under a calm sky, with traces of mist on the lower land to the north of the Wall.

Well-earned refreshments beneath a beautiful rainbow at Sycamore Gap.

The approach to Sycamore Gap from Highshield Crags.

Winter sunrise at Sycamore Gap.

63

The interior of Milecastle 39.

Looking east over Milecastle 39 (Castle Nick) towards a misty Crag Lough, on a late summer morning.

A late summer evening at Milecastle 39, with remnants of internal buildings visible within the milecastle interior.

An early autumn morning on Peel Crags, looking over Milecastle 39, with traces of mist clinging to the distant Crag Lough.

Looking along Peel Crags early on a hazy summer morning, with sunlight accentuating the vegetation precariously clinging to the face of the crags.

Peel Crags, Highshield Crags and Hotbank Crags under a bright orange winter sky, following a light snowfall.

Amazing clarity at Crag Lough and Hotbank Crags after a night of light snow.

Low-lying mist highlighted by early morning light, as the sun rises over Hotbank Crags.

Contrasting winter views of Peel Crags, one with frost and the other with snow, with Crag Lough, Highshield Crags and Hotbank Crags in the distance.

Peel Gap on a winter morning, showing the remains of Peel Gap Tower which was added here presumably to guard the gap. As an extra tower in addition to the two standard turrets between Milecastles 39 and 40, it is unique along the entire course of the Wall; as far as we know, no other Wall miles have anything comparable.

Peel Gap, showing the
Wall and Peel Gap Tower.

Sheep wander through Peel Gap on a
cold December night, many of them
keeping to the footpath!

Contrasting winter morning views over Peel Gap.

A cold and very frosty winter morning at Steel Rigg, with an amazing view across South Tynedale to the distant North Pennines.

Thick fog south of Steel Rigg, with the North Pennines in the distance.

A winter morning at Steel Rigg, looking south towards the distant North Pennines.

This picture was heavily over-processed to replicate the style of esteemed landscape artist John Martin, born locally in Haydon Bridge in 1789. Martin's style was greatly influenced by the vast and rugged landscapes of Northumberland.

Sheep gather at Steel Rigg on a bright morning after a night of heavy frost, perhaps to enjoy the dramatic view through Peel Gap.

Early morning mist flows over Peel Crags.

Early morning mist gives a red glow to the sunlight at Steel Rigg, with dense fog beneath Peel Crags.

A spectacular sunrise at Steel Rigg.

A breathtakingly beautiful panorama after heavy snowfall, looking east from Steel Rigg.

A circular walk starting at Steel Rigg follows the farm track to Hotbank Farm. It continues south to the interesting and fascinating Vindolanda Roman Fort and Museum. The walk continues to The Sill, the Northumberland National Park Centre, and finally back to the Steel Rigg car park.

Vindolanda

Many people find Vindolanda to be the most amazing of all the fascinating Roman sites to be seen in Hadrian's Wall country. It lies 1.5km south of the Wall, on the line of the Stanegate, the Roman road between Carlisle and Corbridge. Thanks to the hard work of the Vindolanda Trust, and hundreds of student and volunteers diggers over recent decades, extensive excavated and consolidated remains of the Roman fort and adjacent vicus (civil settlement) can be seen. In fact there were nine forts here, each built on top of its predecessor. The earliest of these, dating from the late first century, were of timber, replaced eventually by the third/fourth-century stone fort, the remains of which can be seen today. In addition to the fort, ruins of a bath-house, workshops, shops, a tavern, and temples can be visited. There are also full-scale replicas of short stretches of Hadrian's Wall. At its busiest, Vindolanda may have been home to 1,000 soldiers and perhaps 3,000 civilians. After the end of Roman rule, people continued to live here through into the ninth century, but then the site seems to have been abandoned. No visit to Vindolanda is complete without a tour of the magnificent onsite museum which displays a huge array of objects from the excavations, including a selection of the famous writing tablets.

Looking north-west over the replica sections of Hadrian's Wall towards and a golden sunset.

Looking west over Vindolanda during a spectacular winter sunrise.

A view from below Winshield Crags towards the mist-enveloped Peel Crags and Highshield Crags.

A clear winter dawn seen from Winshield Crags, looking towards Hotbank Crags.

Looking east from the bottom of Winshield Crags towards the distant, sunlit Sewingshields Crags.

A lone walker in a spectacular monochromatic winter landscape.

A breathtaking combination of thick overnight frost and dense fog along the line of Peel Crags, Highshield Crags and Hotbank Crags.

Early on a sunny late winter morning, sheep, seemingly oblivious of the cold, begin to stir.

A winter morning of exceptional clarity, with snow showers hurried along on the blustery wind.

A hazy summer sunrise seen from Winshield Crags.

The top of Winshield Crags with the clouds racing across the late autumn sky. The clarity of the air emphasises the contrast and intensity of the colours.

A perfect autumn morning on Winshield Crags, as two walkers enjoy the dramatic view over Peel Crags, Highshield Crags, Hotbank Crags and Crag Lough.

The lichen on this boundary wall seems to glow in the early morning spring sun.

The trig point atop Winshield Crags is the highest point on Hadrian's Wall, at 345m OD. For those walking the Wall, it is close to the halfway point.

It looks as if some ancient deity is pointing the finger of destruction at the Nine Nicks of Thirlwall.

A view over Bogle Hole towards a magnificent sunset. The foundations of the Wall are overlain here by a field wall. Bogle Hole enjoys a sinister reputation, for which there is no real evidence. The origin of the name is lost in time, but in the local dialect a 'bogle' is a ghost or spirit. The remnants of a line of buildings, thought to be medieval or post-medieval shielings (occupied by shepherds during the summer months), survive here, but it is not known whether they relate in any way to the placename.

The Wall and Turret 41a (Caw Gap) covered in a blanket of snow.

Sunrise beneath heavy, threatening clouds, seen from Caw Gap.

A splendid winter sunrise seen from above Caw Gap, looking over South Tynedale towards the distant North Pennines.

The rising winter sun beautifully illuminates the south face of the Wall at Caw Gap.

The sun sets through the haze of a warm summer evening, seen from high on Cawfields Crags.

Thorny Doors on a warm summer evening.

Thorny Doors and Cawfields Crags
on a cool early spring evening.

The Wall weaves its way through a beautiful autumnal landscape down towards Cawfields Quarry.

Looking east along the line of the Wall on Cawfields Crags, with the dead-straight earthworks of the Vallum clearly visible to the south.

Looking north-west from Cawfields Crags, towards a late summer sunset.

A dramatic autumn sunrise at Milecastle 42 (Cawfields).

On a blustery spring morning, the low sun highlights the stonework of Milecastle 42.

Cawfields Quarry. The Alston Limestone Company was given permission to create a quarry at this location in the first half of the last century, resulting in the destruction of a dramatic section of Hadrian's Wall. However, the water filled quarry is now in itself an attractive landscape feature, here reflecting a beautiful sunrise. Cawfields Quarry is sheltered from all artificial light and is officially recognised as a dark sky discovery site, amongst the best in the UK.

From Mucklebank Turret
(Turret 44b) the view west over
Walltown Crags is spectacular.

Turret 45a on Walltown Crags, on a
cool misty spring morning.

Sheep grazing on a peaceful spring
morning at Turret 45a.

Looking south across Turret 45a,
towards the North Pennines.

Turret 45a (Walltown Crags) following a spectacular August downpour, with a stunning double rainbow.

Just to the east of the site of Turret 45b is a steep dip in the course of Hadrian's Wall known as a 'nick'. These nicks were formed as glacial meltwaters drained away as the planet returned to a warmer phase.

A picture of tranquility on an early spring morning on Walltown Crags. I could see the potential of getting closer. The approaching apparition of a strange hooded creature with heavy tripod, bags, lenses and cameras was too much for all but one of the sheep, which beat a rapid retreat. Thankfully the one that remained …..

..... enabled me to take one of my favourite shots. This graphic image incorporates so much about Hadrian's Wall: dramatic crags, the sky, the Wall itself, hill farming, peacefulness and solitude.

One of the iconic features of Hadrian's Wall's central section is the constant climbing and descending along the line of the Whin Sill, as illustrated in this view of Walltown Crags.

An early spring morning on Walltown Crags; the sheep are already engaged in their daily consumption of grass.

Beautifully clear early winter sunsets seen from Walltown Crags.

Walkers approaching the top
of Walltown Crags.

The dawn sky is stunningly reflected within Walltown Quarry. The quarry, which operated through until 1976, destroyed a substantial length of the Wall, but following extensive landscaping it is now a popular country park.

The striking ruins of the thirteenth-century Thirlwall Castle, near Greenhead. The castle was constructed using stone recycled from the Wall and probably also from the nearby fort of Carvoran.

HADRIAN'S WALL
CUMBRIA

Looking east along the longest unbroken still-visible stretch of the Wall, at Birdoswald, early on a spring morning.

Ruins of the eastern abutment of the bridge that carried Hadrian's Wall across the River Irthing. Due to erosion of its banks, the river's course has shifted significantly since Roman times.

Hadrian's Wall and its accompanying National Trail footpath make their way through Willow Bank Farm, down to the ruins of the bridge abutment and the tree-covered banks of the River Irthing beyond.

Birdoswald

Birdoswald fort sits above the Irthing valley to the south, over which it enjoys splendid views. It was originally built to straddle the turf wall, but when this was rebuilt in stone it was realigned to pass north of the fort; subsequently the fort was expanded to that the Wall bonded with its north-west and north-east corners. Today, much of the fort's defensive wall can be seen, standing up to twelve courses high, along with three of its four main gates. Impressive remains of huge granaries can be seen within the fort. Two large post-Roman timber halls were built on the site of the granaries, demonstrating high-status occupation here in the fifth century, following the end of Roman rule. Buried remains of a very extensive vicus (civil settlement) have been recorded by geophysical survey east and west of the fort, no sign of which can be seen on the ground surface.

The long section of Hadrian's Wall east of Birdoswald fort on a winter evening.

A cold winter sunset at Birdoswald.

A perfect autumn morning at Birdoswald. The wooden pillars set into the ruins of the fort's northern granary represent the posts of a large post-Roman timber hall, demonstrating occupation here in the fifth century, following the end of Roman rule.

The Wall west of Birdoswald, on a misty autumn morning.

Turret 51a (Piper Syke) beneath a towering summer sky.

114

Turret 52a (Banks East) under a dramatic autumn sunrise, looking south over the valley of the River Irthing.

Looking east past Turret 52a towards the site of Pike Hill Tower (a signal-tower predating the Wall) on the horizon.

Lanercost Priory incorporates much Roman masonry, recycled from Hadrian's Wall which passes just 1km to the north. Originally founded in 1169 and now largely ruinous, its original nave is still maintained as the local parish church.

This substantial fragment of the Wall, partly reconstructed in the nineteenth century, can be seen at Hare Hill, north-east of Lanercost.

The red sandstone of the priory glows in an autumn sunrise.

The Roman fort at Bewcastle was constructed as an outpost fort, linked by a road with Birdoswald about 10km to the south-east. Uniquely hexagonal in plan, corresponding to the shape of the low hill on which it was built, it is now partly overlain by the ancient church of St Cuthbert, the ruins of a substantial medieval castle, and the extensive buildings of a present-day farm.

The Church of St Cuthbert at Bewcastle was largely rebuilt in Victorian times, but dates back at least as far as the thirteenth century and possibly much earlier. The fabulous cross in the churchyard dates from about 700 AD, when it is possible that a small monastery stood here.

The historic town of Brampton lies 3km south of the Wall. Its distinctive octagonal moot hall was built in 1817.

St Martin's church lies within the Roman fort of Brampton Old Church; its cemetery extends over much of the fort interior. This fort lay close to the line of the Stanegate (the Roman road between Carlisle and Corbridge); it was abandoned following the construction of Hadrian's Wall which ran 2km to the north. The church, originally of twelfth-century date, incorporates much recycled Roman masonry. There may well have been an even older church here, but no sign of it has ever been recorded.

This statue of a Border Reiver was erected in 2003 on Scotland Road, Carlisle.

Carlisle

Carlisle has a beautiful city centre overflowing with history. It has been a garrison town since the time of the Roman's when it was the Empire's most northern town. The Tullie House Museum is an excellent venue for the history of Carlisle and surrounding area.

Carlisle Castle's mightily impressive main gate.

The first castle at Carlisle was built in the 1090s; this was replaced by a new stone structure, including the massive keep that still survives today, in the first half of the twelfth century. The castle partly overlies the city's Roman fort. It endured a turbulent history throughout much of the five centuries prior to the Union of the Crowns in 1603, enduring more sieges than any other castle in England.

Carlisle Cathedral was originally built as a monastic church in 1122, becoming the cathedral for the newly created diocese of Carlisle in 1133. It is a beautiful building with a fascinating history.

PATERNOSTER ROW

123

This modern statue of Edward I stands in Burgh by Sands near the Greyhound Inn. It was erected in 2007 to mark the 700th anniversary his death on the nearby Solway marshes, after which his body was laid in St Michael's Church before being transported south for burial in Westminster Abbey.

This memorial to King Edward I, built in 1685, supposedly marks the place of his death, from dysentery in 1307, aged 68, while preparing yet another invasion of Scotland. It stands on the salt marshes of the Solway Firth, in sight of the nation the so-called 'Hammer of the Scots' was ultimately unable to conquer. Perhaps he should have followed Hadrian's lead, and settled on a northern border rather than obsessing about conquering all that lay beyond.

The mouth of the old Carlisle Canal, at Port Carlisle on the Solway. Constructed in 1823 to facilitate the transport of coal and other goods to and from Carlisle, the canal had a short life, being replaced by a railway in 1854.

The grand manor-house known as Drumburgh Castle, built largely of Roman stone recycled from Hadrian's Wall, dates originally from 1307, though it has been much-altered over sequent centuries. Drumburgh was the smallest fort on the line of the Wall.

This journey began at Wallsend, at the east end of Hadrian's Wall, close to where the River Tyne meets the North Sea; it ends here, where the Wall's west end now lies buried within the sand at Bowness-on-Solway.

Although Hadrian's Wall ended at Bowness-on-Solway, a network of forts and roads extended southwards around the Cumbrian coast, to protect against seaborne invasion. This extended as far south as the fort at Ravenglass, where today the ruins of the bath-house can be seen standing to a height of nearly four metres; they are claimed to be the tallest still-standing Roman walls in Britain.

The remote fort at Hardknott, spectacularly sited high in the Lake District to guard the road linking Ambleside and Ravenglass, reminds us that in addition to Hadrian's Wall there are many other Roman sites to enjoy on the northern fringes of the once-mighty empire.